IT'S NOT OUR MONEY

A BALANCED, BIBLICAL PERSPECTIVE OF WEALTH

DEBORAH B. VOGELZANG

IT'S NOT OUR MONEY – A BALANCED, BIBLICAL PERSPECTIVE OF WEALTH
ISBN 978-163901047-9
Copyright © 2022. All rights reserved

Published by Adoration Press
PO Box 1966, Branson, Missouri 65615

CONTENTS

DEDICATION

To *"The Benefactor"*
and *"The Nine"* +One:

Let us never forget the responsibility of the divinely orchestrated stewardship that has been squarely placed upon our shoulders.

May we be ever mindful: It is *NOT* our money!

PREFACE

When it comes to writing about money, I would consider myself to be the least likely of any to do such a work. Yet here I sit, heart overflowing with truths gleaned over the years. I would be remiss if I did not share with those who might have ears to hear.

I believe there is a great possibility for what many have termed an *end-time transfer of wealth.* The body of Christ could be on the verge of a huge influx of finances. If this is true, then I have a deep concern for *the church* as we know it.

Are we really prepared for such a thing? Yes, there are many great and precious promises regarding the days directly ahead. And yes, I firmly believe that God wants each one of His children to walk in the fullness of His blessings (including but not limited to finances). Yet, if we do not judge ourselves, many in the church as we know it could stumble under the weight of the deceitfulness of riches.

> ***Matthew 13:22*** *– The seed that fell among the thorns represents those who hear God's word, but all too quickly the message is*

> *crowded out by the worries of this life and the lure of wealth, so no fruit is produced.*

Don't get me wrong. The days ahead could be wonderful for those who live in pursuit of God. There is coming a move of His Spirit that will cause every other outpouring to pale in comparison. Days of awakening are upon us!

The LORD has promised that the earth will be filled with His glory. He has promised that His church, His beloved bride will be glorious. God watches over His word to perform it. It shall surely come to pass.

There is a remnant of believers who still hunger and thirst for righteousness. In fact, there are many who still chase after the fire of God as if it were the most precious commodity on earth. But, how do we get from the point *where we are now* to the point of *glorious*? In many cases, the answer would be *only by the grace of God.*

No doubt we are living in the last of the last days. End-time events are standing at the door. Right in the middle of what seems to be the beginning of a global meltdown, there are deep rumblings about something major transpiring in the realms of money – the likes of which have not been seen before.

Proverbs 13:22 – A good man leaves an inheritance to his children's children, but the wealth of the sinner is stored up for the righteous. (NKJV)

What many anticipate to be the answer to all of our troubles could end up being the beginning of a great falling away. Our money system is so deeply entrenched in cycles of debt, many would not know what do if they were suddenly released from the bondage of it.

There is nothing more brutal than church congregations fighting for control of money. And nothing so sad as to see a powerful man or woman of God overtaken by greed or envy.

The only way to navigate such new territory would be based in an intimate relationship with the LORD and His Word, keenly tuned in to the Holy Spirit's wisdom and direction.

If we thought weathering a global pandemic was bad, wait until the body of Christ has more money than it knows that to do with. We've not seen anything yet!

If these things are true. If there really is coming a great influx of money into the hands of God's people, then let us be found preparing our hearts by fully immersing ourselves in the Word of God. There are volumes of scripture on the topic of money, the surface of which we can only begin to touch with this book.

Psalm 119:11 – *I have hidden your word in my heart, that I might not sin against you.*

Ecclesiastes 2:26 – *God gives wisdom, knowledge, and joy to those who please him. But if a sinner becomes wealthy, God takes the wealth away and gives it to those who please him...*

~~~~~~~~~~~~~~~~~~~~~~~~~~~~~

Mark 4:18-20 – *18 The seed that fell among the thorns represents others who hear God's word, 19 but all too quickly the message is crowded out by the worries of this life, the lure of wealth, and the desire for other things, so no fruit is produced. 20 And the seed that fell on good soil represents those who hear and accept God's word and produce a harvest of thirty, sixty, or even a hundred times as much as had been planted!"*

Numbers 14:21 – *But as surely as I live, and as surely as the earth is filled with the LORD's glory*

Isaiah 6:3 – *They were calling out to each other, "Holy, holy, holy is the LORD of*

Heaven's Armies! The whole earth is filled with his glory!"

Isaiah 60:1 – *Arise, shine; For your light has come! And the glory of the LORD is risen upon you. (NKJV)*

Habakkuk 2:14 – *For the earth will be filled with the knowledge of the glory of the LORD, As the waters cover the sea. (NKJV)*

Matthew 5:6 – *Blessed are those who hunger and thirst for righteousness, for they shall be filled. (NKJV)*

Ephesians 5:27 – *He did this to present her to Himself as a glorious church without a spot or wrinkle or any other blemish. Instead, she will be holy and without fault.*

Jeremiah 1:12 – *And the LORD said, "That's right, and it means that I am watching, and I will certainly carry out all my plans."*

Jeremiah 1:12 – *Then the LORD said to me, "You have seen well, for I am ready to perform My word." (NKJV)*

13

INTRODUCTION

Why write a book titled, "It's not our money?"

A healthy perspective of wealth is to never really take ownership of it:

> *Psalm 24:1* – *...The earth is the LORD's, and everything in it. The world and all its people belong to Him.*

> *Psalm 89:11* –*The heavens are Yours, and the earth is Yours; everything in the world is Yours--You created it all.*

> *Psalm 50:10* – *For all the animals of the forest are Mine, and I own the cattle on a thousand hills.*

As we pass through this life on earth, we step into the LORD's pasture and He is the Shepherd of it. We must know that when we depart this life, we take nothing with us. The wealth of this world remains here long after we have moved into eternity.

At best, caretakers and stewards we are, servants of the Father and His dear Son, our LORD and Master, Jesus Christ.

Good & Faithful Servants

Matthew 25:14-30 *– 14 "Again, the Kingdom of Heaven can be illustrated by the story of a man going on a long trip. He called together his servants and entrusted his money to them while he was gone. 15 He gave five bags of silver to one, two bags of silver to another, and one bag of silver to the last--dividing it in proportion to their abilities. He then left on his trip.*

16 "The servant who received the five bags of silver began to invest the money and earned five more. 17 The servant with two bags of silver also went to work and earned two more. 18 But the servant who received the one bag of silver dug a hole in the ground and hid the master's money.

19 "After a long time their master returned from his trip and called them to give an account of how they had used his money. 20 The servant to whom he had entrusted the five bags of silver came forward with five more and said, 'Master, you gave me five bags of silver to invest, and I have earned five more.'

21 "The master was full of praise. 'Well done, my good and faithful servant. You have been faithful in handling this small amount, so now I will give you many more responsibilities. Let's celebrate together!'

22 "The servant who had received the two bags of silver came forward and said, 'Master, you gave me two bags of silver to invest, and I have earned two more.'

23 "The master said, 'Well done, my good and faithful servant. You have been faithful in handling this small amount, so now I will give you many more responsibilities. Let's celebrate together!'

24 "Then the servant with the one bag of silver came and said, 'Master, I knew you were a harsh man, harvesting crops you didn't plant and gathering crops you didn't cultivate. 25 I was afraid I would lose your money, so I hid it in the earth. Look, here is your money back.'

26 "But the master replied, 'You wicked and lazy servant! If you knew I harvested crops I didn't plant and gathered crops I didn't cultivate, 27 why didn't you deposit my money in the bank? At least I could have gotten some interest on it.'

28 "Then he ordered, 'Take the money from this servant, and give it to the one with the ten bags of silver. 29 To those who use well what they are given, even more will be given, and they will have an abundance. But from those who do nothing, even what little they have will be taken away. 30 Now throw this useless servant into outer darkness, where there will be weeping and gnashing of teeth.' (NLT)

Each one of these servants had his own perspective of the master. Two proved themselves trustworthy and diligent – each a good manager. The third servant had a skewed idea of the master and proved himself to be unwise in the choices he made about the assignment.

Regardless of their success, regardless of their perspective, in the end, none of it was their money. Every resource at their disposal belonged the master. He simply asked them to put it to work and bring increase to his domain. They were given responsibility and tested as to the effectiveness of their stewardship.

It was not their money. It belonged to the Master.

~~~~~~~~~~~~~~~~~~~~~~~~~~~~~~

Very often, in the Gospels we will find similar stories from slightly different perspectives. It may be the same story yet recounted differently, depending upon the details recalled by the writer; or it could be such that Jesus told the same illustration in a different way on two separate occasions. Regardless, Luke's account of the previous parable is slightly different. We are presenting it here for additional consideration:

Luke 19:11-26 – The crowd was listening to everything Jesus said. And because he was nearing Jerusalem, he told them a story to correct the impression that the Kingdom of God would begin right away. 12 He said, "A nobleman was called away to a distant empire to be crowned king and then return. 13 Before he left, he called together ten of his servants and divided among them ten pounds of silver, saying, 'Invest this for me while I am gone.' 14 But his people hated him and sent a delegation after him to say, 'We do not want him to be our king.'

15 "After he was crowned king, he returned and called in the servants to whom he had given the money. He wanted to find out what their profits were. 16 The first servant reported, 'Master, I invested your money and made ten times the original amount!'

17 "'Well done!' the king exclaimed. 'You are a good servant. You have been faithful with the little I entrusted to you, so you will be governor of ten cities as your reward.'

18 "The next servant reported, 'Master, I invested your money and made five times the original amount.'

19 "'Well done!' the king said. 'You will be governor over five cities.'

20 "But the third servant brought back only the original amount of money and said, 'Master, I hid your money and kept it safe. 21 I was afraid because you are a hard man to deal with, taking what isn't yours and harvesting crops you didn't plant.'

22 "'You wicked servant!' the king roared. 'Your own words condemn you... 23 why didn't you deposit my money in the bank? At least I could have gotten some interest on it.'

24 "Then, turning to the others standing nearby, the king ordered, 'Take the money from this servant, and give it to the one who has ten pounds.'

25 "'But, master,' they said, 'he already has ten pounds!'

26 "'Yes,' the king replied, 'and to those who use well what they are given, even more will be given. But from those who do nothing, even what little they have will be taken away...'"

LEST WE FORGET

Deuteronomy 8:11-14, 17-18 – 11 "Beware that you do not forget the LORD your God by not keeping His commandments, His judgments, and His statutes which I command you today, 12 lest – when you have eaten and are full, and have built beautiful houses and dwell in them; 13 and when your herds and your flocks multiply, and your silver and your gold are multiplied, and all that you have is multiplied; 14 when your heart is lifted up, and you forget the LORD your God who brought you out of the land of Egypt, from the house of bondage; ...

17 "then you say in your heart, 'My power and the might of my hand have gained me this wealth.' 18 And you shall remember the LORD your God, for it is He who gives you power to get wealth, that He may establish His covenant which He swore to your fathers, as it is this day. (NKJV)

The passage is clear. The purpose for wealth is so that *God* may use it to establish His kingdom; to fulfill the promises He has made to mankind.

How will God do that? Through you and I. Money doesn't just fall out of the heavens. No. He puts resources into our hands for His purpose and plans.

This passage is also a warning: Don't forget Who gave you these wonderful things; don't forget why He brought you to this place in time.

Furthermore, it is a charge to remember the journey of those who came to possess the promise. In other words, don't forget what previous generations went through to bring us into the blessings of God:

> *Deuteronomy 8:15-16* - *15 "who led you through that great and terrible wilderness, in which were fiery serpents and scorpions and thirsty land where there was no water; who brought water for you out of the flinty rock; 16 "who fed you in the wilderness with manna, which your fathers did not know, that He might humble you and that He might test you, to do you good in the end. (NKJV)*

The old-timers used to say, *"Wouldn't take nothing for the journey."*

The challenge with generational wealth is that younger generations have not endured the journey. Figuratively speaking, they have not wandered in the wilderness for 40 years. The test is not multi-generational – only the blessing.

Without character development and education, it leaves a door gaping open for corruption. This is why the children of Israel were commissioned to tell it to their children and their children's children. If they wanted to continue to walk in the blessings of God, the lessons of the previous generations could not be lost.

Forgetfulness is the downfall of many peoples. The Israelites were strongly admonished not to forget the journey and the experiences that taught them along the way. It is good to remember the price paid by previous generations and learn from their mistakes.

A modern-day proverb comes to mind:

Those who fail to learn from history are destined to repeat it.

There is no way to retain blessing without thoroughly engaging the next generation in the previous journey. Thoroughly examining the covenants that govern it are equally important.

A Heavenly Perspective

> *Matthew 6:20-21 – 20 "but lay up for yourselves treasures in heaven, where neither moth nor rust destroys and where thieves do not break in and steal. 21 "For where your treasure is, there your heart will be also. (NKJV)*

> *Matthew 12:35 –"A good man out of the good treasure of his heart brings forth good things, and an evil man out of the evil treasure brings forth evil things. (NKJV)*

Jesus said it best: laying up heavenly treasure is far more important than the riches of this world. We must keep an eternal perspective. Wealth in this life is fleeting and corruptible.

Yes, we can do good with money. In many respects it is good to have money in this life… as long as money does not control us. No matter how much we possess, if we do not know the LORD Jesus Christ, we are spiritually bankrupt. (To know the LORD means to have an intimate, personal relationship with Him; to know Him is to love Him.)

> *Matthew 6:33 – Seek the Kingdom of God above all else, and live righteously, and he will give you everything you need.*

We must keep these things in perspective if we want to be effective for God.

The Corruption of Money

As previously stated, we must not allow future generations to forget the journey of those who have gone before. If the past is forgotten, the door is wide open for corruption to sneak in like a thief.

In our society today, money equals power. And this type of power can be quite addictive. If we want to keep corruption in check, it is so important to remind ourselves and future generations that "It's not our money."

> *1 Timothy 6:10 – For the <u>love</u> of money is the root of all kinds of evil. And some people, craving money, have wandered from the true faith and pierced themselves with many sorrows.*

It's not money that is evil. It is the LOVE of money that corrupts. We must keep our motives under constant scrutiny or lust for power can quickly spiral out of control. Greed, envy and all sorts of evil rush in to overtake. Thus, sorrow upon sorrow follows far too often.

No, wealth is not the answer – just ask the rich about the poor state of their children. Not everyone who is wealthy has problems with their heirs, but the challenges seem to get more complicated as the generations pass.

Most people long to leave riches to their children so they won't have to endure the hardships their parents and grandparents went through. Nevertheless, in order to retain the blessing, the subsequent generations must understand the trials and mistakes, the suffering and the sorrows.

There is no testimony without a test; no preservation without perseverance.

No, the journey must be remembered – not just by the elders, but by those who come after. We must teach our children to love and honor God. Elsewise they will love money more than the One from Whom the blessings come.

> **Proverbs 11:28** – *Trust in your money and down you go! But the godly flourish like leaves in spring.*

Only God and the relationship we have with Him will keep us on a sure path.

Parable of The Lost Son

One of the most powerful illustrations Jesus tells is the story most commonly known as *"The Prodigal Son."* It is a wonderful story about the love of a father and his willingness to forgive his son regardless of his mistakes. Though most people don't really think about the root cause in the story line, it is worth noting here.

The wayward son was enticed into a lifestyle of sin when he was granted his inheritance. There was clearly a secret desire to sin hidden in his heart – that, coupled with a lack of maturity to handle what was granted, made for a devastating scenario.

Luke 15:11-13, 17-24 – 11 "...A man had two sons. 12 The younger son told his father, 'I want my share of your estate now before you die.' So, his father agreed to divide his wealth between his sons. 13 "A few days later this younger son packed all his belongings and moved to a distant land, and there he wasted all his money in wild living...

17 "When he finally came to his senses, he said to himself, 'At home even the hired servants have food enough to spare, and here I am dying of hunger! 18 I will go home to my father and say, "Father, I have sinned against both heaven and you, 19 and I am no longer worthy of being called your son. Please take me on as a hired servant."'

20 "So he returned home to his father. And while he was still a long way off, his father saw him coming. Filled with love and compassion, he ran to his son, embraced him, and kissed him. 21 His son said to him, 'Father, I have sinned against both heaven and you, and I am no longer worthy of being called your son.'

22 "But his father said to the servants, 'Quick! Bring the finest robe in the house and put it on him. Get a ring for his finger and sandals for his feet.

23 And kill the calf we have been fattening. We must celebrate with a feast, 24 for this son of mine was dead and has now returned to life. He was lost, but now he is found...'

Thank God for the redemptive work of Christ and a loving Father who receives us with open arms, even when we've made a mess of things.

We should seek God diligently when it comes to granting an inheritance to our children. Are they ready for it? Can they handle the responsibility, or will they be tempted to blow it on a sinful lifestyle?

A word to the wise should be sufficient. Yes, there is forgiveness available, but let's do everything we can to avoid heart-breaking circumstances. The prodigal's father thought his son was dead. With so much sin abounding all around us, we'll need to be super-vigilant to protect the next generation; to teach them the way they should go (Proverbs 22:6).

Will they make mistakes? Likely. Did we make mistakes? Absolutely. Is forgiveness available? Most assuredly.

Again, thank God for His mercy and love!

~~~~~~~~~~~~~~~~~~~~~~~~~~~~

Proverbs 22:6 – Direct your children onto the right path, and when they are older, they will not leave it.

Numbers 14:30-34 – 30 You will not enter and occupy the land I swore to give you. The only exceptions will be Caleb… and Joshua… 31 'You said your children would be carried off as plunder. Well, I will bring them safely into the land, and they will enjoy what you have despised… 33 And your children will be like shepherds, wandering in the wilderness for forty years. In this way, <u>they will pay for your faithlessness</u>, until the last of you lies dead in the wilderness. 34

Because your men explored the land for forty days, you must wander in the wilderness for forty years – a year for each day, suffering the consequences of your sins. Then you will discover what it is like to have me for an enemy.'

Luke 12:34 - *Wherever your treasure is, there the desires of your heart will also be.*

Luke 6:45 – *A good person produces good things from the treasury of a good heart, and an evil person produces evil things from the treasury of an evil heart. What you say flows from what is in your heart.*

Luke 12:31 – *Seek the Kingdom of God above all else, and he will give you everything you need.*

John 6:27 – *But don't be so concerned about perishable things like food. Spend your energy seeking the eternal life that the Son of Man can give you. For God the Father has given me the seal of his approval."*

Prophetically speaking of Jesus...

Isaiah 53:9 – *And they made His grave with the wicked... with the rich at His death... (NKJV)*

WHY PROSPER?

3 John 2 – *Beloved, I pray that you may prosper in all things and be in health, just as your soul prospers. (NKJV)*

Proverbs 10:22 - *The blessing of the LORD makes one rich, and He adds no sorrow with it. (NKJV)*

For the Good

Matthew 25:35-40, 45 – *35 For I was hungry, and you fed me. I was thirsty, and you gave me a drink. I was a stranger, and you invited me into your home. 36 I was naked, and you gave me clothing. I was sick, and you cared for me. I was in prison, and you visited me.'*

37 "Then these righteous ones will reply, 'Lord, when did we ever see you hungry and feed you? Or thirsty and give you something to drink? 38 Or a stranger and show you hospitality? Or naked and give you clothing? 39 When did we ever see you sick or in prison and visit you?'

40 "And the King will say, 'I tell you the truth, when you did it to one of the least of these my brothers and sisters, you were doing it to me!'

45 ...'I tell you the truth, when you refused to help the least of these my brothers and sisters, you were refusing to help me.'

***James 2:14-16** –14 What good is it, dear brothers and sisters, if you say you have faith but don't show it by your actions? Can that kind of faith save anyone? 15 Suppose you see a brother or sister who has no food or clothing, 16 and you say, "Good-bye and have a good day; stay warm and eat well"-- but then you don't give that person any food or clothing. What good does that do?*

***1 John 3:16-19** – 16 We know what real love is because Jesus gave up his life for us. So, we also ought to give up our lives for our brothers and sisters. 17 If someone has enough money to live well and sees a brother or sister in need but shows no compassion--how can God's love be in that person?*

18 Dear children, let's not merely say that we love each other; let us show the truth by our actions. 19 Our actions will show that we belong to the truth, so we will be confident when we stand before God.

Proverbs 11:25 – *The generous soul will be made rich, and he who waters will also be watered himself. (NKJV)*

Why prosper? There are many reasons. *"Blessed to be a blessing"* is right at the top of the list.

What About the Poor?

It seems as though in recent years, we've heard a lot of back channel communications about the alleviation of poverty. There are people in certain positions of power that believe poverty can be completely eradicated in the earth and have set their sights on doing just that. While that might be a noble cause, we want to pause and remember what the scripture says on this issue:

Matthew 26:11 – *"You will always have the poor among you...*

Deuteronomy 15:11 – *There will always be some in the land who are poor. That is why I am commanding you to share freely with the poor...*

What About Lending?

Luke 6:32-36 – *32 "If you love only those who love you, why should you get credit for that? Even sinners love those who love them! 33 And if you do good only to those who do good to you, why should you get credit? Even sinners do that much! 34 And if you lend money only to those who can repay you, why should you get credit? Even sinners will lend to other sinners for a full return.*

35 "Love your enemies! Do good to them. Lend to them without expecting to be repaid. Then your reward from heaven will be very great, and you will truly be acting as children of the Most High, for he is kind to those who are unthankful and wicked. 36 You must be compassionate, just as your Father is compassionate.

We're still talking about doing good.

Toxic Charity

All that being said, it is important to interject the need for wisdom in our charitable activities.

Proverbs 4:5 – *Get wisdom; develop good judgment. Don't forget my words or turn away from them.*

Proverbs 16:16 – *How much better to get wisdom than gold, and good judgment than silver!*

34

Proverbs 23:23 – Get the truth and never sell it; also get wisdom, discipline, and good judgment.

There is an old proverb that says:

Give a man a fish and he will eat for a day; teach a man to fish and he will eat for a lifetime.

Some types of charity tend to foster dependence. For example, food pantries that offer staple items at no charge often see familiar faces each week (the same repeat customers over and over). Sadly, those same people visit similar outreaches in various locations. Over time, such activity can evolve into hoarding situations.

Food insecurity is no laughing matter and we want to bring comfort to those who need it. Nonetheless, when recipients have stockpiled so much food that it rots on the shelf, that could be considered toxic charity – especially if the food is given to them with no fees or questions asked.

A never-ending cycle of dependence almost always evolves into toxicity. It is important to support a lifestyle of independence, even among the needy. We want those who are suffering to be able to maintain a certain level of dignity. Additionally, people tend to put more value on something if they have made some sort of investment, whether that be a small fee or some sort of labor exchange.

Community gardens teach skills that help the poor become more independent. Feeding programs that require a small fee offer a hand *up* as opposed to a *hand-out*. Another good example of non-toxic benevolence would be the *Habitat for Humanity* model.[1] Participants get homes for a fraction of the cost, but they have invested enough in the process to learn valuable life lessons.

Why prosper? So, we can give to the poor, lend to those in need, and do good. We must put action to our faith by making a willful choice to be a blessing.

It's not our money.

~~~~~~~~~~~~~~~~~~~~~~~~~~~~~~

Mark 14:7 – *You will always have the poor among you, and you can help them whenever you want to…*

John 12:8 – *You will always have the poor among you…*

---

[1] https://www.habitat.org/

DISPENSATIONAL PATTERNS

For the next few chapters we will take a closer look at the biblical idea of wealth transfer. If this is truly ordained by God, then surely there will be some evidence of it in the Bible?

We firmly believe in divine provision and prosperity in this, *the age of grace*. However, in examining end-time literature, there are no clear indicators on the matter of wealth transfer at the end of the age. However, there are patterns throughout history that suggest such an event. The only way to dig it out is by taking a deep dive into dispensational theology which supports such an idea. We will do what we can to keep it simple.

Most believers never hear the word *dispensation* unless they go to Bible school. For the novice, it is a big word that carries little meaning. It can take many years of study and practice to have a firm grasp of the topic.

Simply put, a dispensation is a period of time that could be referred to as an *age.* It is usually used in direct reference to the God/mankind relationship (i.e. How God has dealt with man through the ages, at various times and in various ways).

For example, we are currently living in what theologians call the *age of grace* – a time when belief in the redemptive work of Christ puts us in right-standing with God. Never before in history could man be cleansed from sin and become a new creature in Christ. We are saved by grace (also known as being born again by the Holy Spirit). It is a time when the salvation and free favor of God profusely abound.

> *2 Corinthians 5:17 – Therefore, if anyone is in Christ, he is a new creation; old things have passed away; behold, all things have become new.*

> *Ephesians 2:8 – God saved you by his grace when you believed. And you can't take credit for this; it is a gift from God.*

> *John 3:3 – Jesus replied, "I tell you the truth, unless you are born again, you cannot see the Kingdom of God."*

> *Luke 4:19 – To proclaim the accepted and acceptable year of the Lord [the day when*

salvation and the free favors of God profusely abound].[2]

These periods of time hold several factors in common. We could call them *patterns*:

- An opening event
- God defines His expectations of mankind, which usually involves a healthy dose of believing and obeying.
- Mankind inevitably fails. We have a perpetual tendency to move in the opposite direction from what God requires.
- Each age offers an avenue for redemption – most often involving grace on God's part and faith on the part of mankind.
- A closing event – which chiefly involves some form of judgment

Those are the primary indicators of dispensational patterns. Upon those parameters, nearly every Bible scholar can agree. However, there are other patterns that are not as easy to identify. We will discuss those in more detail as we go, but for now let's look a little closer at the designations.

Here's a quick list of seven:

- The Age of Innocence (Genesis chapters 1 through 3)
- The Age of Conscience (Genesis chapters 4 through 7)
- The Age of Government (Genesis chapters 8 through 11)
- The Age of Promise (Genesis chapter 12 through Exodus chapter 2)
- The Age of the Law (Exodus chapter 19 through the destruction of Jerusalem, 70 A.D.)
- The Age of Grace (Acts chapter 1 through the Great Tribulation)
- The Kingdom Age (The Millennial Reign of Christ which officially starts with the Second Coming of Christ and ends with the final judgment of Satan and his cohorts.)

It is sometimes easier to define the patterns in the better-known storylines because there is simply more detail in the Bible. The earlier time periods... well, there are only a few chapters to study. Whereas, later in the Bible, we have volumes of information.

Let's take a closer look...

GAPS & OVERLAPS

First of all, we'll make the point that lines are somewhat blurred between the end of one dispensation and the beginning of the next.

Here is a list of beginnings:

- God creates man – the Age of Innocence
- Cain murders Abel – the Age of Conscience
- God establishes a new covenant with Noah – the Age of Government
- God calls Abram – the Age of Promise
- Israel agrees to keep the law – the Age of the Law
- Christ ascends / sends the Holy Spirit – the Age of Grace
- Christ returns as Conquering King – the Kingdom Age

Here is a list of endings:

- Expulsion from Eden – the Age of Innocence
- The Great Flood – the Age of Conscience
- The Tower of Babel – the Age of Government
- The Bondage of Egypt – the Age of Promise
- The Fall of Jerusalem (70 A.D.) – the Age of Law
- The Great Tribulation – the Age of Grace

- Final Judgment / Lake of Fire – the Kingdom Age[3]

To our point, there seems to be a bit of a *gap* between the end of *the age of innocence* and the beginning of *the age of conscience*. There is also an unspecified period of time between the Tower of Babel (*the age of government*) and the call of Abram (also known as Abraham) (*the age of promise*).

On the other hand, it could be noted that some dispensations took several years to fully transition into a new age. In these cases, early signs of the next age started before the previous one was finished. We will call that *overlap.*

The overlap of *the age of promise* to *the age of the law* is likely the longest. Most theologians agree there seems to be two distinct acts of judgment before the final close of that dispensation.

The first started with a severe famine, resulting in God's chosen people departing the land of promise and then being left in slavery in Egypt for 400 years (Exodus chapters 1 and 2). The second judgment was of Egypt itself, including the ten plagues (Exodus chapters 7 through 12),

---

3   https://gbible.org/wp-content/uploads/2016/07/Chart-of-the-Dispensation.pdf

the departure of their workforce, and a final blow at the parting of the Red Sea (Exodus 14:26-31)

As another example, *the age of grace* officially began with the church in Acts chapter 1. However, the transition started with the birth of Christ and before. Here we see an *overlap*. Additionally, according to most theological schools of thought, the end of *the dispensation of the law* didn't officially wrap up until the destruction of Jerusalem in 70 A.D. – long after the official start of the church age.

> *Matthew 23:37-39* – *37 "O Jerusalem, Jerusalem, the city that kills the prophets and stones God's messengers! How often I have wanted to gather your children together as a hen protects her chicks beneath her wings, but you wouldn't let me. 38 And now, look, your house is abandoned and desolate. 39 For I tell you this, you will never see me again until you say, 'Blessings on the one who comes in the name of the LORD!'"*

There are two age changes yet to come: the end of *the age of grace* and the completion of *the kingdom age*, one-thousand years later. We may very well live to see the last days of this dispensation unfold before our very eyes.

Some are wondering, *"What about the Tribulation?"* It is marked by most scholars as being a special 7-year period of judgment that is the culmination of all the preceding ages. It begins with the revelation of the antichrist and ends with Satan and his cohorts' utter defeat.[4] Like an exclamation mark, it punctuates the end of *the age of grace.*

The Tribulation is destined to be one of the greatest gap-fillers of all time. There are many schools of thought as to the timing. This author tends to believe that the church will be gone in the rapture before the tribulation officially begins.

> *1 Thessalonians 4:13-18* – *13 And now, dear brothers and sisters, we want you to know what will happen to the believers who have died so you will not grieve like people who have no hope. 14 For since we believe that Jesus died and was raised to life again, we also believe that when Jesus returns, God will bring back with him the believers who have died. 15 We tell you this directly from the Lord: We who are still living when the Lord returns will not meet him ahead of those who have died. 16 For the Lord*

---

[4] https://gbible.org/wp-content/uploads/2016/07/Chart-of-the-Dispensation.pdf

himself will come down from heaven with a commanding shout, with the voice of the archangel, and with the trumpet call of God. First, the Christians who have died will rise from their graves. 17 <u>Then, together with them, we who are still alive and remain on the earth will be caught up in the clouds to meet the Lord in the air.</u> Then we will be with the Lord forever. 18 So encourage each other with these words.

Even now, we see early indicators of the antichrist spirit already busy at work in the earth. This age transition will be colossal, marked with several things we will discuss in later chapters.

Until then, there is a little more to explore about dispensations.

Transition Teams

It could be noted that with each new dispensation there is a cast of characters that oversee the switch. In most cases, when an age ends with judgment, God raises up a man (or team of individuals) – a changing of the guard, so-to-speak.

Noah and his family are a great example. The sin and disobedience of mankind had reached an unredeemable level of abomination. God could only find one man righteous enough to oversee the transition. God identified Noah ahead of time and asked him to build a boat. When judgment came at the end of the age (Genesis 7), Noah and his family sailed into history, preserving a legacy passed down from the patriarchs of old.

In *the dispensation of the law*, Moses and his siblings were the transition team. This transition from *the age of promise* took 80+ years to complete.

Jesus Himself was the overseer of the transition to *the age of grace*. It took no less than 33 years. While he taught His disciples as those living under Mosaic law, He prepared them to be apostles in the next dispensation – the ones who would administer the most significant age change in history.

We're talking about dispensational patterns. Yes, there are opening and closing events. And God has distinct ways of dealing with mankind in every age. Nevertheless, consider this: one thing most theologians overlook is the subject of wealth.

It's in there. We just have to look for it.

~~~~~~~~~~~~~~~~~~~~~~~~~~~~~~~

Prophetically speaking of Jesus...

> ***Isaiah 53:12*** *– Therefore I will divide Him a portion with the great, <u>and He shall divide the spoil with the strong</u>, because He poured out His soul unto death, and He was numbered with the transgressors, and He bore the sin of many, and made intercession for the transgressors. (NKJV)*

WEALTH TRANSFER

Careful study reveals that each dispensation is marked by some sort of wealth (very often during opening or closing events):

Adam entered *the age of innocence* being given the responsibility over all of creation; he left the dispensation inheriting a planet that was now under the curse of the fall. It still had great potential, though resources were now limited by the corruption of sin.

The age of conscience ended with the judgment of the great flood. Noah basically inherited the earth and the fullness thereof at the beginning of *the age of government*.

God called Abram (Abraham) to go to a place he did not know – to a land of *promise* – to possess it as his own. In his lifetime, because of his obedience and great faith, Abraham amassed tremendous wealth. Eventually, what was left of his multigenerational abundance was carried away into Egypt by his great-grandchildren (the children of Jacob also known as Israel).

When the Israelites departed Egypt (after 400 years of slavery), they carried away Egyptian wealth as plunder.

Exodus 3:21-22 – 21 "And I will give this people favor in the sight of the Egyptians; and it shall be, when you go, that you shall not go empty-handed. 22 But every woman shall ask of her neighbor, namely, of her who dwells near her house, articles of silver, articles of gold, and clothing; and you shall put them on your sons and on your daughters. So, you shall plunder the Egyptians." (NKJV)

Psalm 105:37 – He also brought them out with silver and gold, and there was none feeble among His tribes. (NKJV)

Let's take a moment to consider how the children of Israel handled this unique inheritance.

What was the first thing they did? They made an idol of gold and gave themselves over to all sorts of despicable sin in the worship thereof. Then judgment came and 3,000 men fell by Levitical swords.

Exodus 32:27-28 – Moses told them, "This is what the LORD, the God of Israel, says: Each of you, take your swords and go back and forth from one end of the camp to the other. Kill everyone--even your brothers, friends, and neighbors." 28 The Levites obeyed Moses' command, and about 3,000 people died that day.

Eventually, the children of Israel got it right and used a portion of the wealth to build the tabernacle. Finally, a way was established to worship the One true God – the God of Abraham, Isaac and Jacob.

Upon Israel's commitment to keep the God's laws, a new age was born with a promise to once again inherit a land flowing with milk and honey. The only stipulations were faith (trust) and obedience. *The dispensation of the law* ended approximately 1,500 hundred years later with the destruction of Jerusalem and a scattering of the Jews to the four corners of the earth (70 A.D.).

The transition to *the age of grace* started with the birth of Christ. Wise men from the east carried with them the wealth of a king and presented it to Him not long thereafter. Additionally, there was a wealth transfer in the early church as believers sold their possessions and laid the proceeds at the apostles' feet.

Now we are faced with another age change. With it will surely come another transfer of wealth. At this time, there is a lot of mystery and secrecy associated with even the thought of it.

Some hope it will happen in our lifetime, while others remain skeptical.

The Storehouses of Joseph

We have already established that there was a two-fold judgment and a 400-year ending to *the age of promise*. There is another model within the dispensation that deserves a closer look. We should take some time to consider the storehouses of Joseph.

Joseph's story marks the beginning of the end of *the age of promise*. Notably, there are fourteen chapters beginning in Genesis chapter 37 primarily devoted to Joseph and his story. That's a lot of documentation compared to Abraham and the other patriarchs. If it was not important, God would not have taken the time to give such attention to detail.

Joseph's calling in life was to preserve a nation. He was a dreamer and an interpreter, as well as being divinely gifted as an administrator.

Pharaoh of Egypt had been warned by God about a devastating time of famine to come – dreams which Joseph interpreted. Pharaoh subsequently put Joseph in charge of the entire land of Egypt. He was tasked with building storehouses and overseeing a time of plenty in preparation for what was to come.

> *Genesis 41:38-41 – 38 So Pharaoh asked his officials, "Can we find anyone else like this man so obviously filled with the spirit of God?" 39 Then Pharaoh said to Joseph, "Since God has revealed the meaning of the dreams to you, clearly no one else is as intelligent or wise as you are. 40 You will be in charge of my court, and all my people will take orders from you. Only I, sitting on my throne, will have a rank higher than yours." 41 Pharaoh said to Joseph, "I hereby put you in charge of the entire land of Egypt."*

Of particular note (a point that is most concerning) is Joseph's leadership during the time of famine:

> *Genesis 47:13-21 – 13 Meanwhile, the famine became so severe that all the food was used up, and people were starving throughout the lands of Egypt and Canaan. 14 By selling grain to the people, <u>Joseph eventually collected all the money in Egypt and Canaan,</u> and <u>he put the money in Pharaoh's treasury</u>. 15 When the people of Egypt and Canaan ran out of money, all the Egyptians came to Joseph. "Our money is*

gone!" they cried. "But please give us food, or we will die before your very eyes!"

16 Joseph replied, "<u>Since your money is gone, bring me your livestock</u>. I will give you food in exchange for your livestock." 17 So they brought their livestock to Joseph in exchange for food. In exchange for their horses, flocks of sheep and goats, herds of cattle, and donkeys, Joseph provided them with food for another year.

18 But that year ended, and the next year they came again and said, "<u>We cannot hide the truth from you, my lord. Our money is gone, and all our livestock and cattle are yours. We have nothing left to give but our bodies and our land.</u> 19 Why should we die before your very eyes? Buy us and our land in exchange for food; <u>we offer our land and ourselves as slaves for Pharaoh</u>. Just give us grain so we may live and not die, and so the land does not become empty and desolate."

20 So <u>Joseph bought all the land of Egypt for Pharaoh. All the Egyptians sold him their fields because the famine was so severe, and soon all the land belonged to Pharaoh.</u> 21 <u>As for the people, he made them all slaves, from one end of Egypt to the other.</u>

Joseph led in a time of dire circumstances. Who could have done it any better? Sadly, it is worth noting that he administered decisions that resulted in slavery for *two* entire nations at that time – Egypt and Israel. Abraham's descendants were not free from that bondage for 400 years.

If wealth is coming at the end of this age, and if the patterns of the Bible hold true, then some sort of judgment will likely be on its heels. If God is raising up individuals to be caretakers of His storehouses (in this the last of the last days), it might not be just for a glorious time of plenty.

It should also be noted that we are now living in a different dispensation. Joseph lived in *the time of promise.* We live in *the age of grace.* In it, God deals differently with mankind. Everything is now subject to the redemptive work of Christ.

For believers, we are not appointed unto wrath (1 Thessalonians 5:9 KJV). The judgment of the nations will be one thing, but for those in the ark of safety (the church of the LORD Jesus Christ), we will likely be delivered out of the great wrath or tribulation to come.

1 Thessalonians 5:1-10 – 1 Now concerning how and when all this will happen, dear brothers and sisters, we don't really need to write you. 2 For you know quite well that the day of the Lord's return will come unexpectedly, like a thief in the night. 3 When people are saying, "Everything is peaceful and secure," then disaster will fall on them as suddenly as a pregnant woman's labor pains begin. And there will be no escape.

4 But you aren't in the dark about these things, dear brothers and sisters, and you won't be surprised when the day of the Lord comes like a thief. 5 For you are all children of the light and of the day; we don't belong to darkness and night. 6 So be on your guard, not asleep like the others. Stay alert and be clearheaded. 7 Night is the time when people sleep and drinkers get drunk. 8 But let us who live in the light be clearheaded, protected by the armor of faith and love, and wearing as our helmet the confidence of our salvation.

9 <u>For God chose to save us through our Lord Jesus Christ, not to pour out his anger on us.</u> 10 Christ died for us so that, whether we are dead or alive when he returns, we can live with him forever.

THE AGE OF GRACE

We have already noted the wealth of a king being transferred to Jesus around the time of His birth. Many believe his earthly father, Joseph, used at least part of the treasure to pay for the family's escape to Egypt.

> *Matthew 2:13-15* – *13 After the wise men were gone, an angel of the Lord appeared to Joseph in a dream. "Get up! Flee to Egypt with the child and his mother," the angel said. "Stay there until I tell you to return, because Herod is going to search for the child to kill him." 14 That night Joseph left for Egypt with the child and Mary, his mother, 15 and they stayed there until Herod's death. This fulfilled what the Lord had spoken through the prophet: "I called my Son out of Egypt."*

There is a line of thought that the wise men brought with them much more than trinkets. Some believe that it was a portion of the wealth of Israel that had been carried off to the East during the time of the Babylonian captivity.

Still others believe that Daniel had left instructions with the astrologers to watch for the sign of the star. That means the lessons he taught would have been passed down for hundreds of years before their journey – and a treasure laid up for a king during that time.

There's not a lot written concerning these things, so we can't be dogmatic about it. Simply stated: they came from the east with generous gifts:

> **Matthew 2:9-11** – *9 … the wise men went their way. And the star they had seen in the east guided them to Bethlehem. It went ahead of them and stopped over the place where the child was. 10 When they saw the star, they were filled with joy! 11 They entered the house and saw the child with his mother, Mary, and they bowed down and worshiped him. Then <u>they opened their treasure chests and gave him gifts of gold, frankincense, and myrrh</u>.*

The Early Church

As far as the early church is concerned, there are indicators of additional wealth transfers just at *the church age* was getting started:

> **Acts 2:42-47** – *42 All the believers devoted themselves to the apostles' teaching, and to fellowship, and to sharing in meals*

(including the Lord's Supper), and to prayer.

43 A deep sense of awe came over them all, and the apostles performed many miraculous signs and wonders. 44 And all the believers met together in one place and shared everything they had. 45 <u>They sold their property and possessions and shared the money with those in need.</u> 46 They worshiped together at the Temple each day, met in homes for the Lord's Supper, and shared their meals with great joy and generosity-- 47 all the while praising God and enjoying the goodwill of all the people. And each day the Lord added to their fellowship those who were being saved.

Acts 4:32-35 – *32 All the believers were united in heart and mind. And <u>they felt that what they owned was not their own,</u> [...not our money...] so they shared everything they had. 33 The apostles testified powerfully to the resurrection of the Lord Jesus, and God's great blessing was upon them all. 34 <u>There were no needy people among them, because those who owned land or houses would sell them 35 and bring the money to the apostles to give to those in need.</u>*

Ananias & Sapphira

And then the deceitfulness of riches made a grand gesture:

Acts 5:1-11 – 1 But there was a certain man named Ananias who, with his wife, Sapphira, sold some property. 2 He brought part of the money to the apostles, claiming it was the full amount. With his wife's consent, he kept the rest.

3 Then Peter said, "Ananias, why have you let Satan fill your heart? You lied to the Holy Spirit, and you kept some of the money for yourself. 4 The property was yours to sell or not sell, as you wished. And after selling it, the money was also yours to give away. How could you do a thing like this? You weren't lying to us but to God!"

5 As soon as Ananias heard these words, he fell to the floor and died. Everyone who heard about it was terrified. 6 Then some young men got up, wrapped him in a sheet, and took him out and buried him.

7 About three hours later his wife came in, not knowing what had happened. 8 Peter asked her, "Was this the price you and your husband received for your land?" "Yes," she replied, "that was the price."

9 And Peter said, "How could the two of you even think of conspiring to test the Spirit of the Lord like this? The young men who buried your husband are just outside the door, and they will carry you out, too."

10 Instantly, she fell to the floor and died. When the young men came in and saw that she was dead, they carried her out and buried her beside her husband. 11 Great fear gripped the entire church and everyone else who heard what had happened.

If they were living in *the age of grace*, why would such an act of judgment be issued so fiercely and quickly? Ananias and Sapphira were supposedly believers. Wasn't the blood of Jesus and grace of God enough to cover their sin?

Where was the mercy of God? Well, He had more to think about than just those two. And their demise might have been the greatest act of mercy the LORD could have administered at the time. Not only for their sake, but for the sake of everyone else, too.

We would like to believe Ananias and Sapphira went to heaven (because they believed in Jesus). In the least, it is clear that the consequences of their actions brought them into eternity a little sooner than expected.

Technically, they got in trouble for lying to the Holy Spirit. Yet in reality, <u>they were lying about money</u>. Remember, the love of money is the <u>root</u> of all evil (1 Timothy 6:10).

The move of God in the early church was holy. There was great love and unity among the people. It was a time of purity and sanctification. There was no room for the Holy Spirit to allow that sort of corruption to infiltrate the church at that time – not deception, and certainly not the love of money.

If glory is coming to the body of Christ – purity, unity, and holiness – there will be no room for the corruption of money. We must keep our hearts pure before the LORD.

We're talking about dispensational patterns. If we are believing for this great end-time transfer of wealth, the LORD would say unto us, *"Be careful what you wish for."*

Remember, it's not our money.

He's not playing church anymore. It's time to get serious about the things of God.

I have heard modern-day prophets declare that the days of Ananias and Sapphira would visit the church once again. If that is true, surely there is a pattern of such a thing in other dispensations.

~~~~~~~~~~~~~~~~~~~~~~~~~~~~~~

Even though this chapter is about *the age of grace*, we're going to interrupt for a moment. We want to take a quick look back into *the age of the law* for an important dispensational pattern:

The Valley of Trouble

The seventh chapter of Joshua contains a heart-breaking tale about an event that took place relatively early in the dispensation. Not long after the children of Israel had begun the process of reclaiming the land of promise, someone's hidden agenda of greed caused a great upheaval.

Joshua had specifically instructed God's people not to touch any of the wealth of Jericho.

> *Joshua 6:16-17 – 16 ...Joshua commanded the people... 17 Jericho and everything in it must be completely destroyed as an offering to the LORD...*

However, there was sin the camp:

> *Joshua 7:1 – But Israel violated the instructions about the things set apart for the LORD. A man named Achan had stolen some of these dedicated things, so the LORD was very angry with the Israelites.*

One man's secret sin was attributed to the entire camp of Israel. Yes, Achan took something that was not his, but all of Israel was held accountable for the iniquity.

No one else in the camp knew anything was wrong until they were defeated in their next military campaign. The people of Ai sent them on the run, with 36 Israeli soldiers killed in action. (Joshua 7:2-9) When Joshua sought the Lord for an answer, the Lord told him that someone had broken the covenant and gave strict instructions about what to do next. (Joshua 7:10-15).

Eventually Achan was singled out as the guilty party (Joshua 7:18).

> *Joshua 7:19-21 –19 Then Joshua said to Achan, "My son, give glory to the LORD, the God of Israel, by telling the truth. Make your confession and tell me what you have done. Don't hide it from me."*
>
> *20 Achan replied, "It is true! I have sinned against the LORD, the God of Israel.*

21 Among the plunder I saw a beautiful robe from Babylon, 200 silver coins, and a bar of gold weighing more than a pound. I wanted them so much that I took them. They are hidden in the ground beneath my tent, with the silver buried deeper than the rest."

Joshua 7: 24-26 *– 24 Then Joshua and all the Israelites took Achan, the silver, the robe, the bar of gold, his sons, daughters, cattle, donkeys, sheep, goats, tent, and everything he had, and they brought them to the valley of Achor. 25 Then Joshua said to Achan, "Why have you brought trouble on us? The LORD will now bring trouble on you." And all the Israelites stoned Achan and his family and burned their bodies. 26 They piled a great heap of stones over Achan... That is why the place has been called the Valley of Trouble ever since. So, the LORD was no longer angry.*

How would the story of Achan compare to the account of Ananias and Sapphira?

- Both events happened *early* in a new dispensation
- Both situations involved the corruption of money: with Ananias and Sapphira, it was the deceitfulness of riches; with Achan it was greed.

65

- Both events brought rapid judgment because the Lord could not allow such sin to take root among His people at that state of the dispensation.

Joshua, God's ordained leader at the time, had given specific instruction as to what should be done with the spoils of Jericho. Everything was to be destroyed as an offering to the Lord. Yet, God's instruction through Joshua had not been taken seriously. Achan didn't think the rules applied to him. Greed got the upper hand and it cost him everything.

~~~~~~~~~~~~~~~~~~~~~~~~~~~~~~

This is a good segue back into *the age of grace.* Let's take a little closer look at managing money and God's ordained leadership for the body of Christ.

New Covenant Protocols

Today, in considering the possibility of another wealth transfer, we are still technically living in *the age of grace*, subject to the protocols of the New Testament. Dispensational patterns have been established from the beginning of the age.

Even though we know it's not ours, let's ask this question:

What are we going to do with our money?

For those who do not have a plan, for those who want to be good stewards but lack direction from the LORD... In this dispensation, the model could be heavily connected to apostles.

Why apostles? Because they see the big picture and they know where the need is greatest. They can help direct our giving in a wise manner because they are anointed with apostolic grace. (See in the final chapter, the section of scriptures labeled *"Apostolic Grace."*)

Remember, the early church laid their wealth at the feet of the apostles for distribution to the needy.

We're not suggesting that we are required to donate *everything* we have. No such guidelines have been declared. The early church simply *chose* to do as their hearts directed; they *chose* to give it all. It might not be a bad model, but the admonition here is to *follow our hearts.*

It should be noted that every believer can and should be led by the Holy Spirit in their giving. There will be times when there is wisdom in seeking the input of apostles. Again, they see the big picture. They know the LORD's heart and are gifted to administer from an apostolic point of view. Apostles are intended by God to be our partners for stewarding His plans in this dispensation.

How do we find an apostle when very few carry the title? A true apostle is a leader of leaders, one who advances the troops from behind, and seldom has a need to be addressed as such. A true apostle is likely one sent by God to guide a particular group of people, raised up as an overseer in cities, regions and/or nations.

If we ask the LORD, He will direct us to the council we need.

Remember: It's not our money.

~~~~~~~~~~~~~~~~~~~~~~~~~~~~

Romans 8:14 - *For all who are led by the Spirit of God are children of God.*

WHAT CAN WE EXPECT?

Prophetically speaking, there are several things the body of Christ can expect to transpire before the end of this age – *the age of grace.* This chapter is not an exhaustive teaching on the subject of end-times, but rather a glimpse as to how wealth might impact certain events.

That means we're not going to discuss the tribulation, other than to say – we can't take our money with us when we go. By the time the church makes it's exit, we'll be singing *Que Sera Sera, "Whatever will be, will be..."*

In a previous chapter we briefly discussed *Transition Teams.* Yes, Jesus was the primary facilitator of the age change, but there were a few other voices that directly preceded His appearing that are worth mentioning now. They were not His disciples, but they had a voice that still rings loud and clear in the scriptures – and even into this next transition.

Let us consider John the Baptist. He preceded the first coming of Christ. When he came onto the scene, he came in the spirit and power of Elijah (see *Spirt of Elijah* in *Scriptures for Meditation*).

As we close out this dispensation, for as much time as we have left, it is the church of the LORD Jesus Christ that will be operating in the spirit of Elijah. Why? Because we, the church, are numbered among the forerunners for Jesus' *second* coming.

The second set of voices just prior to Christ's first appearing were people of prayer. Two of the most notable figures are mentioned in Luke chapter 2. Their names were Simeon and Anna.

> **Luke 2:25-38** – *25 At that time there was a man in Jerusalem named Simeon. He was righteous and devout and was eagerly waiting for the Messiah to come...28 Simeon was there. He took the child in his arms and praised God, saying, 29 "Sovereign Lord, now let your servant die in peace, as you have promised. 30 I have seen your salvation, 31 which you have prepared for all people. 32 He is a light to reveal God to the nations, and he is the glory of your people Israel!"... 36 Anna, a prophet, was also there in the Temple....37...She never left the Temple but stayed there day and night, worshiping God with fasting and prayer. 38 She came along just as Simeon was talking with Mary and Joseph, and she began praising God. She talked about the*

child to everyone who had been waiting expectantly for God to rescue Jerusalem.

History tells us that as they were looking for the advent of the Messiah. They gave themselves regularly to prayer. Do not discount the importance of these people in the transition of the age. Likewise, do not discount the importance of prayer in this next shift.

Even now, God has already been raising up intercessors across the globe who are given to prayer about future, end-time events. I personally know of at least one prayer group that took time during the pandemic of 2020-21 to address such things. In those weekly prayer sessions, the LORD commissioned them to address three main topics:

- The Apostacy (2 Thessalonians 2:3)
- An End-Time Harvest of Souls (James 5:7-8)
- The Glorious Bride (Ephesians 5:27)

We're still talking about wealth and wealth transfer. And all three of those topics are connected in one way or another to money.

Now for a deeper dive ...

Apostacy

First, let's define apostacy:

- "Abandonment of religion, the ancient criminal offense of heresy or non-belief in religion."[5]
- "An act of refusing to continue to follow, obey, or recognize a religious faith."[6]
- "A defection or revolt."[7]
- "A defection from truth; falling away, forsake."[8]

In speaking of dispensational patterns, it is easy to understand that each age is marked with a departure from faith. In the beginning it started with individuals, but as the population increased, so did the size of the segment that fell away. Think about it, Noah and his family were the only ones who survived the first great apostacy.

God requires faith and obedience. Those who do not comply eventually come under judgment. Why? Because they defect from the truth. This is what theologians call *apostacy*.

---

[5] https://www.wordnik.com/words/apostacy
[6] https://www.merriam-webster.com/dictionary/apostasy
[7] https://en.wikipedia.org/wiki/Apostasy
[8] https://www.blueletterbible.org/lexicon/g646/kjv/tr/0-1/

In considering this current dispensation, it is horrifying to think there will still be those who could walk away from the truth of Jesus as LORD. Yet, there it is, plainly written:

> **2 Thessalonians 2:3** – *Let no one deceive you by any means; for that Day will not come unless the <u>falling away</u> comes first, and the man of sin is revealed, the son of perdition (NKJV)*

A quick look at the text in its original language (Greek), indicates clearly that there will be those who willfully chose to reject or turn away from the Lordship of Jesus Christ. Sadly, they will set themselves upon a broad path toward forsaking the things of God.

I once worked for a highly respected minister who believed and taught that the only pre-requisite for eternal life is to receive Jesus as LORD and Savior. To be considered *rapture ready* is to be *born again.* I tend to agree with this theology. Yet in nearly every dispensation, *falling away* or *apostacy* is a common pattern.

Hopefully, the apostacy of this age will not be among those who are truly born-again. Instead it could be a reference to those who have a form of godliness but deny its power.

> ***2 Timothy 3:1-5*** *– 1... in the last days there will be very difficult times. 2 For people will love only themselves and their money. They will be boastful and proud, scoffing at God, disobedient to their parents, and ungrateful. They will consider nothing sacred. 3 They will be unloving and unforgiving; they will slander others and have no self-control. They will be cruel and hate what is good. 4 They will betray their friends, be reckless, be puffed up with pride, and love pleasure rather than God. 5 <u>They will act religious, but they will reject the power that could make them godly</u>. Stay away from people like that!*

To be clear, the pattern of the ages is set, and there will be those who fall in line with those who go down to the pit:

> ***Isaiah 38:18*** *– For Sheol cannot thank You, Death cannot praise You; Those who go down to the pit cannot hope for Your truth.*

We must save as many as we can.

How does wealth fit into this equation? Think of the wealth of Egypt and how it brought corruption right into the Israelite camp. Idolatry of a *golden* calf was the first order of business. If the dispensational pattern holds true and a transfer of wealth happens once again, some sort of apostasy is surely on its heels.

2 Peter 3:10 – But the day of the Lord will come as unexpectedly as a thief... and the earth and everything on it will be found to deserve judgment.

End-Time Harvest of Souls

2 Peter 3:9 – The Lord isn't really being slow about His promise, as some people think. No, He is being patient for your sake. <u>*He does not want anyone to be destroyed, but wants everyone to repent.*</u>

James 5:7-8 – 7 Dear brothers and sisters, be patient as you wait for the Lord's return. Consider the farmers who patiently wait for the rains in the fall and in the spring. They eagerly look for the valuable harvest to ripen. 8 You, too, must be patient. Take courage, for the coming of the Lord is near.

Matthew 24:14 – And the Good News about the Kingdom will be preached throughout the whole world, so that all nations will hear it; and then the end will come.

Having been in the ministry and around other believers nearly every day for many decades, it becomes easy to be *"churchy"* in our manner of speaking. Not everyone thinks this way. Therefore, we want to take some time to ponder.

One of the key elements of the timing of last day events has to do with what has been commonly termed, *a great harvest of souls.* When reflecting about the pandemic prayer group mentioned earlier in this chapter, this one topic dominated at least 75% of their prayer sessions.

We will not see the face of Jesus Christ again until this gospel has been preached to every tribe in every nation. That is a tall order for the body of Christ. It is our great commission:

> ***Matthew 28:18-20*** – *18 Jesus came and told his disciples, "I have been given all authority in heaven and on earth. 19 Therefore, go and make disciples of all the nations, baptizing them in the name of the Father and the Son and the Holy Spirit. 20 Teach these new disciples to obey all the commands I have given you. And be sure of this: I am with you always, even to the end of the age."*

An end-time awakening to God will likely precede the rapture of the church (also known as the catching away of the saints). And in the process, surely the bride will become more glorious.

A large portion of believers in America are sitting in their pews waiting for Jesus to come for them. While He is waiting for them to go to a lost and dying world.

Before we make the next points, we want to make note that God is well able to do what He needs to do to empower the church for the assignment. He owns the cattle on a thousand hills (Psalm 50:10), right?

> **Isaiah 59:1** – *Surely the arm of the LORD is not too short to save, nor his ear too dull to hear. (NIV)*[9]

However, when it comes to bringing in the precious fruit of the earth (James 5:7-8), money could possibly be a factor. It is true where God guides, He provides. Yet, it is foolish to think that we won't need money to bring in the harvest.

---

[9] Scripture quotations marked (NIV) are taken from the Holy Bible, New International Version®, NIV®. Copyright © 1973, 1978, 1984, 2011 by Biblica, Inc.™ Used by permission of Zondervan. All rights reserved worldwide.

The farmer understands it takes money to bring in a crop. Machinery must be maintained. Barns must be built, fuel bought and crews fed. A wise farmer plans in advance for such expenses.

There is no time during the harvest to do anything but harvest. No banking. No cashing out at the grain elevator. There is only a small window of time in which the harvest can be gathered. In the that window, money must already be set aside.

> *John 4:35-38 – 35 You know the saying, 'Four months between planting and harvest.' But I say, wake up and look around. The fields are already ripe for harvest. 36 The harvesters are paid good wages, and the fruit they harvest is people brought to eternal life. What joy awaits both the planter and the harvester alike! 37 You know the saying, 'One plants and another harvests.' And it's true. 38 I sent you to harvest where you didn't plant; others had already done the work, and now you will get to gather the harvest."*

If there is truly going to be a great in-gathering of souls, then it only stands to reason that there could also be a transfer of wealth that precedes it. As with every other dispensation, there could be overlaps and/or gaps in the order of events as we close out the age. Logically, the transfer of wealth might come toward the beginning of the end. Time will tell.

When it comes, it could trigger some into apostacy. It could finance laborers into ripe and ready harvest fields. And likely, at the same time, the body of Christ, His precious bride will begin to take unto herself elements of glory not seen heretofore.

The Glorious Church

As previously stated, the children of Israel eventually got it right. Ultimately, they used the wealth of Egypt to create a primary place of worship. The tabernacle was used for decades (if not centuries) as they wandered through the wilderness and beyond. Of what remained they then carried into the promised land. They were marked and set apart from other nations because of their God-granted affluence.

In the passage of time, along came David and Solomon who amassed great wealth to build for God a temple in the holy city, Jerusalem:

> *1 Kings 6:19-22 – 19 And he prepared the inner sanctuary inside the temple, to set the ark of the covenant of the LORD there. 20 The inner sanctuary... He overlaid it with*

pure gold, and overlaid the altar of cedar. 21 So Solomon overlaid the inside of the temple with pure gold. He stretched gold chains across the front of the inner sanctuary, and overlaid it with gold. 22 The whole temple he overlaid with gold, until he had finished all the temple; also, he overlaid with gold the entire altar that was by the inner sanctuary. (NKJV)

The interior of the temple built by Solomon was overlaid in pure in gold. Not all of that gold came from Egypt, but there is a clear picture that associates wealth with the extravagant worship of Almighty God.

We are blessed to a blessing – not just to the needy – but to Him. It blesses God when we worship Him with what He has given us. Whether out of abundance or out of need, blessing the LORD with what we have is an act of true worship.

1 Corinthians 3:16 – Do you not know that you are the temple of God and [that] the Spirit of God dwells in you? (NKJV)

2 Corinthians 6:16 – And what agreement has the temple of God with idols? For you are the temple of the living God. As God has said: "I will dwell in them and walk among them. I will be their God, and they shall be My people." (NKJV)

Ephesians 2:21-22 *– 21 in whom the whole building, being fitted together, grows into a holy temple in the Lord, 22 in whom you also are being built together for a dwelling place of God in the Spirit. (NKJV)*

Ephesians 5:25-27 *– 25 ... just as Christ loved the church. He gave up His life for her 26 to make her holy and clean, washed by the cleansing of God's word. 27 He did this to present her to Himself as a glorious church without a spot or wrinkle or any other blemish. Instead, she will be holy and without fault.*

As noted, the interior of the first temple and its furnishings were overlaid with pure gold. Now, in this dispensation, believers in the LORD Jesus Christ, are considered the temple – because we have the Holy Spirit within.

Assuredly, we are a spiritual house, but when the church is caught away, she will be glorious in every way – ever mindful that the wealth of this world pales in comparison to what lies ahead.

We can't take the wealth of this world with us, but that does not mean we won't be abundantly blessed as we go – prosperous in every way.

Remember, one of the most precious commodities on earth, paves the streets in heaven.

> *2 Corinthians 4:6-7 – 6 ...God who commanded light to shine out of darkness, who has shone in our hearts to give the light of the knowledge of the glory of God in the face of Jesus Christ. 7 But we have this treasure in earthen vessels, that the excellence of the power may be of God and not of us. (NKJV)*

ARE WE READY?

If there really is an end-time transfer of wealth coming, I suppose the million-dollar question would be, *"How?"* Some think they know. Others don't have a clue.

As with any other dispensation-changing event, it would certainly behoove us to invest time in praying about it. In due season, the LORD will have His way in these things.

The best thing we can do is prepare our hearts. We want to make certain that we learn from the mistakes of previous ages and generations, leaving no room for the enemy to stick his foot in the door of our treasuries.

Early in this book we introduced the topic of corruption, warning against the evil of riches. Now, we'll point forward to the chapter of the book called, *"Scriptures for Meditation." "The Corruption of Wealth"* is the first section with dozens of scriptures to bring the point home.

God is not against His people having money. As a matter of fact, we firmly believe that he wants his servants to prosper. We believe in the spiritual law of sowing and reaping and pray that each reader comes into a deeper understanding of the responsibility of what it means to be *"blessed to be a blessing."*

As the contents of this book have unfolded, there is a valid concern in this author's heart for what traditionally transpires after a dispensation-changing wealth transfer. We want to make every effort to warn against yielding to a wrong spirit. We don't want anyone to end up on the judgment side of a falling away.

Having been in the ministry for several years, we have seen a thing or two. Most distressing is the damage we can do to one another. When the church yields to disputes over money, it can be staggering to the soul. We have seen the best of friends and colleagues come to irreconcilable differences – always at the expense of the precious ones they serve.

Sadly, no one ever sees it coming. No one ever imagines that money can be such a powerful catalyst for dissolution. Division and strife can enter rather quickly, blind-siding everything and everyone in its wake.

Divide and conquer is the strategy of the enemy. If he can't keep us from being blessed, then he will do everything he can to destroy us in the aftermath. In such cases, no one wins but the devil.

If this great end-time transfer of wealth truly comes to fruition, mark my word, lest we prepare, it could bring unimaginable destruction to the church as we know it. We must not forget the mistakes and warnings of the previous dispensations.

We should all be very watchful as to how we walk, especially if random believers come into massive quantities of wealth.

Toxic charity is a real thing and the last thing the body of Christ needs is more division. Misguided generosity and benevolence could easily spur power struggles no one could have anticipated. Envy and greed can inspire real corruption at the highest levels of leadership. As previously stated, we must be led by the Holy Spirit. We must earnestly seek wisdom and understanding.

> ***James 1:5*** – *If you need wisdom, ask our generous God, and he will give it to you. He will not rebuke you for asking.*

Hear me! And hear me well. An end-time transfer of wealth may not be the answer to all of our problems. If we do not wake up, it could cause more trouble in the church than we ever dreamed. Unless we learn to love each other like the early church, money will not be a unifier. It will be a divider.

The dispensational pattern is clear. After a transfer of wealth, comes judgment for those on the wrong side of it.

> *1 Peter 4:17 – For the time has come for judgment, and it must begin with God's household. And if judgment begins with us, what terrible fate awaits those who have never obeyed God's Good News?*

> *Revelation 2:5 – Look how far you have fallen! Turn back to me and do the works you did at first. If you don't repent, I will come and remove your lampstand from its place among the churches.*

> *1 Corinthians 11:31-32 – 31 But if we would examine ourselves, we would not be judged by God in this way. 32 Yet when we are judged by the Lord, we are being disciplined so that we will not be condemned along with the world.*

We have been warned!

Judge Not

The end of days is quickly approaching. Transfer of wealth or not, we must be careful how we walk:

> **Ephesians 4:1-3** – *I, therefore, the prisoner of the Lord, beseech you to walk worthy of the calling with which you were called, 2 with all lowliness and gentleness, with longsuffering, bearing with one another in love, 3 endeavoring to keep the unity of the Spirit in the bond of peace. (NKJV)*

There is no allowance for envy, jealously, strife or greed in the glorious church:

> **1 Corinthians 13:4-7** – *4 Love is patient and kind. Love is not jealous or boastful or proud 5 or rude. It does not demand its own way. It is not irritable, and it keeps no record of being wronged. 6 It does not rejoice about injustice but rejoices whenever the truth wins out. 7 Love never gives up, never loses faith, is always hopeful, and endures through every circumstance.*

> **Luke 6:37** – *"Judge not, and you shall not be judged. Condemn not, and you shall not be condemned. Forgive, and you will be forgiven. (NKJV)*

There is a distinct possibility that thousands of believers will be stepping into great wealth in the days ahead, many of whom have a limited idea of how to proceed with such a gift.

- They will need our prayer for wisdom.
- Their children will need prayer for protection and the preservation of a generational mandate.

Think of lottery winners. (No, we are not advocating gambling, but we could learn a thing or two from their mistakes.) In the end, only a very few people retain any of their winnings. What could have been multi-generational wealth ends up being squandered because they lack the wisdom to handle it.

Without God in the equation, we all stand to waste whatever blessings come our way.

God forbid all these blessed believers come into grand fortunes only to have their children and grand-children overtaken with the corruption that often accompanies such provision.

What if, from the beginning, those who suddenly come into great wealth were to put God in the equation? What if they were to adopt the phrase: "It's not our money. It's God's"?

1 Peter 5:5-6 –5 ... Yes, all of you be submissive to one another, and be clothed with humility, for "God resists the proud, but gives grace to the humble." 6 Therefore humble yourselves under the mighty hand of God, that He may exalt you in due time,

Now there is a healthier perspective.

It's not our money, is it?

WORKING THE WORD

We have spent several chapters making the case for wealth. But we haven't mentioned much about what we do to position ourselves to receive such blessings. There are spiritual laws that govern this aspect of our lives and we would be wise to understand the protocols.

> ***James 2:26*** *– Just as the body is dead without breath, so also faith is dead without good works.*

How to do we work the word by faith? We work the Word by *doing*, by practicing acts of obedience. We must put action to our faith in order to demonstrate it to the LORD.

Another way to work the Word is to declare it. Sometimes the best way to operate in faith is by *saying.*

> ***Mark 11:22-24*** *- 22 Then Jesus said to the disciples, "Have faith in God. 23 I tell you the truth, you can say to this mountain, 'May you be lifted up and thrown into the sea,' and it will happen. But you must really believe it will happen and have no doubt in your heart. 24 I tell you, you can pray for*

anything, and if you believe that you've received it, it will be yours.

Ephesians 3:20 - *Now to Him who is able to do exceedingly abundantly above all that we ask or think, according to the power that works in us,*

If His Word is hidden in our hearts, there is a power within that we can draw upon – a power to walk in faith – a power to do and to say.

As has already been established, the LORD is the One Who gives us the power to get wealth (Deuteronomy 8:18). He gives us wisdom if we ask for it (James 1:5). He shows us what to do (Romans 8:14).

If we are still seeking direction, we can at least make confessions of faith, for example:

We thank you LORD, that it is You Who give us the power to get wealth. You are showing us what to do and how to do it. We ask LORD that you show us what seed to sow and where to sow it. We ask LORD that you teach us your ways. And we thank you LORD that you take pleasure in the prosperity of your servants. We covenant to use it for Your purposes and ask that you would grant unto your servants to be good stewards for the wealth that you entrust to us. All for Your glory and Your honor!

Remember:

Romans 10:17 – *So then faith [comes] by hearing, and hearing by the word of God. (NKJV)*

Hebrews 11:6 – *And it is impossible to please God without faith. Anyone who wants to come to him must believe that God exists and that he rewards those who sincerely seek him.*

Romans 14:23 – *...If you do anything you believe is not right, you are sinning.*

1 Corinthians 10:31 – *...whatever you do, do it all for the glory of God.*

Sowing & Reaping

Seedtime and harvest is a spiritual law that governs multiple aspects of life on planet earth.

Galatians 6:7 – *"Don't be under any illusion: you cannot make a fool of God! A man's harvest in life will depend entirely on what he sows (The Phillips Translation[10]).*

---

[10] https://ccel.org/bible/phillips/CP09Galatians.htm

The first time the LORD opened my understanding to the above scripture was from a different translation – the same message with a slightly different emphasis:

> **Galatians 6:7** – *Do not be deceived, God is not mocked; for whatever a man sows, that he will also reap. (NKJV)*

As a child in Sunday School this passage was constantly thrown in my face as a threat to do good, to behave like a good girl. *"You better be careful or you will reap what you sow."* In other words, *"If you do bad things, you will reap bad things."*

That line of thinking kept my behavior in check for many self-righteous years of legalism. However, there is an entirely different meaning that should also be applied to the positive side of the equation. *"If you sow good seed in good ground, you're bound to reap a good harvest."*

Many years ago, the LORD actually taught me about this passage. He literally opened my understanding one day to see it in a way I had never seen it before.

When it comes to giving and receiving, very often the enemy of our soul, the purveyor of doubt, comes along with a phrase like this:

"Yeah, that giving stuff, it doesn't work. It may work for others, but it won't work for you."

Or he might say, *"It won't work this time."*

What is that?

That is deception. That is the father of lies (John 8:44) sowing seeds of doubt, mocking God (and His spiritual laws) in the process.

Now let's rehearse that verse again: *"Do not be deceived, God is not mocked! For whatever a man sows, that he will also reap!"*

When the devil tells us a lie, the opposite must be true!

That means it will work! It will work every single time! If we sow good seed in good ground, we will reap a harvest!

Here is the qualifier we often miss:

Romans 8:25 – *But if we hope for that we see not, then do we with patience wait for it. (KJV)*

Hebrews 6:11-12 – *And we desire that each one of you show the same diligence to the full assurance of hope until the end, 12 that you do not become sluggish, but*

95

imitate those who <u>through faith and patience</u> inherit the promises. (NKJV)

Here's one more, for good measure:

Luke 6:38 – *"Give, and it will be given to you: good measure, pressed down, shaken together, and running over will be put into your bosom. For with the same measure that you use, it will be measured back to you." (NKJV)*

First Fruits

The very first type of offering mentioned in the Bible is that of *first fruits*.

Genesis 4:3-4 – *3 When it was time for the harvest, Cain presented some of his crops as a gift to the LORD. 4 Abel also brought a gift--the best of the firstborn lambs from his flock. The LORD accepted Abel and his gift*

Why was Cain's offering not accepted? There is no mention of *first fruits*. It simply says *some of his crops*. God does not want <u>a</u> portion. He likes to receive the FIRST and BEST of our increase.

Abel offered the BEST of the FIRSTBORN lambs. It was the first picture we see of Christ our redeemer – the Lamb of God who takes away the sin of the world (John 1:29).

96

Several months ago, the word of the LORD came unto me saying, *"The fastest way to get to where you're going in the days ahead is with the offering of first fruits."*

We have always been faithful tithers (which we'll discuss in the next section), but I can honestly say, no one had ever challenged us to consider offering *first fruits.*

I had to do a little bit of study.

Basically, to offer *first fruits* is to offer the first (and best) portion of a particular form of increase. For example, at harvest time a farmer might give the first truck load to the LORD.

Here's another example of what would be considered *first fruits*:

> ***Leviticus 19:23-25*** *– 23 "When you enter the land and plant fruit trees, leave the fruit unharvested for the first three years and consider it forbidden. Do not eat it. 24 <u>In the fourth year the entire crop must be consecrated to the LORD as a celebration of praise.</u> 25 Finally, in the fifth year you may eat the fruit. <u>If you follow this pattern, your harvest will increase</u>. I am the LORD your God.*

With this type of giving there is a guarantee of success.

> **Deuteronomy 26:1-2** – 1 *"When you enter the land the LORD your God is giving you as a special possession and you have conquered it and settled there, 2 put some of the first produce from each crop you harvest into a basket and bring it to the designated place of worship--the place the LORD your God chooses for his name to be honored.*

Some may say, *"I am not a farmer. What can I do?"* We could give the first paycheck from a new employer or perhaps give the LORD all the profit made from our first yard sale. Whenever we have a *first* – we should put Him first and, if possible, give the best of it to Him.

For the children of Israel reclaiming the land of promise, their offering of *first fruits* would have been the spoils of Jericho.

Think about Achan and *the Valley of Trouble (*from the chapter on *The Age of Grace). When we first examined Joshua chapter 7, we did not share all the detail about the defeat Israel endured. Sadly, what put them in such a position was a defilement of the *first fruit* offering.

Joshua 7:2-6 – 2 Joshua sent some of his men from Jericho to spy out the town of Ai, east of Bethel, near Beth-aven. 3 When they returned, they told Joshua, "There's no need for all of us to go up there; it won't take more than two or three thousand men to attack Ai. Since there are so few of them, don't make all our people struggle to go up there." 4 So approximately 3,000 warriors were sent, but they were soundly defeated. The men of Ai 5 chased the Israelites from the town gate as far as the quarries, and they killed about thirty-six who were retreating down the slope. The Israelites were paralyzed with fear at this turn of events, and their courage melted away. 6 Joshua and the elders of Israel tore their clothing in dismay, threw dust on their heads, and bowed face down to the ground before the Ark of the LORD until evening.

Israel was expecting the same victory they had enjoyed at Jericho. But because of hidden sin and stealing what was set aside for God, with great dismay, they were defeated. They had expected success.

The broken covenant brought with it a completely different outcome. It was only after repentance and setting things in order that they could once again move forward expecting God to have their backs. They did and He did (Joshua chapter 8).

The offering of *first fruits* is one way for increase to come to us. It's not the only way, but according to what the LORD said to me recently, it may be one of the most effective ways to move forward under His umbrella of blessing.

#

In order to understand tithing, it is best to look at the whole of scripture. Let's start with the children of Israel:

> ***Leviticus 27:30*** *– "One-tenth of the produce of the land, whether grain from the fields or fruit from the trees, belongs to the LORD and must be set apart to him as holy.*

Believers in church should hear on a regular basis that, *"the tithe belongs to the LORD."* It's not something we *pay*. It's something we *return* to its rightful Owner.

Most of us assume that the rest of what we have is ours to do with as we so choose. I suppose there is truth in this assumption. Yet, we should always do our best to remember, *"It's not our money."*

Tithing is a well-establish principle mentioned throughout the dispensations, starting with Abraham in *the age of promise.*

Nothing like tithing will open the windows of heaven for those who dare to put God to the test.

> **Malachi 3:10** – *Bring all the tithes into the storehouse... If you do," says the LORD of Heaven's Armies, "I will open the windows of heaven for you. I will pour out a blessing so great you won't have enough room to take it in! Try it! Put me to the test!*

Failure to practice such an opportunity could cause the believer to miss out on one of the greatest avenues of blessing available in this earth-bound life.

As for me and my house, we have learned the value and discipline of tithing. It's too late to try to convince us otherwise. Such an act of obedience is considered holy and sanctifies the rest of our increase.

God will not force us to tithe. It is, like every other type of giving, a willful choice to be made. But scripture is clear: the tithe belongs to the LORD. It would behoove each of us to present to Him what He declares is His portion. Who are we to steal from Almighty God? In remembrance of Achan, we don't want to be found on the wrong side of that equation.

To be clear, this book is not about tithing or even methods to prosper. It's not about giving and receiving; sowing and reaping. There are plenty of books already written, works which thoroughly cover these topics with excellence.

If anything, this book is primarily about stewardship and keeping a proper perspective about what belongs to God – taking a closer look at His intentions for wealth and riches. Because when His blessings overtake us, rest assured, He has purpose in it.

The purpose of this book is to challenge every reader to take these truths a step further in realizing that <u>everything we have is God's</u>. We are simply to be administrators or managers of what He puts into our hands.

The passages at the beginning of this book remind us that the earth is the LORD's and the fullness thereof.

In the second chapter called, *"Why Prosper?"* We devoted an entire section to doing good with our money.

Alms giving is all about benevolence – doing good by giving to the poor and needy.

Alms is primarily mentioned in the gospels and the books of Acts. Every time Jesus mentions it, the giver is encouraged to do it discreetly, even secretly.

There is no specific mention as to a return on this type of giving. Jesus only mentions *rewards*. He consistently instructs us to give from what we already have. Alms giving is something we do in obedience because He is kind. We are to be His hands extended.

> *Matthew 6:1-4 – 1 Take heed that ye do not your alms before men, to be seen of them: otherwise ye have no reward of your Father which is in heaven. 2 Therefore when thou doest thine alms, do not sound a trumpet before thee, as the hypocrites do in the synagogues and in the streets, that they may have glory of men. Verily I say unto you, they have their reward. 3 But when thou doest alms, let not thy left hand know what thy right hand doeth: 4 That thine alms may be in secret: and thy Father which seeth in secret himself shall reward thee openly. (KJV)*

> **Luke 11:41** – *"But rather give alms of such things as you have... (NKJV)*

> **Luke 12:33** – *"Sell what you have and give alms; provide yourselves money bags which do not grow old, a treasure in the heavens that does not fail, where no thief approaches nor moth destroys.*

In speaking of the benevolence of Cornelius...
> **Acts 10:2, 31** – *2 a devout man and one who feared God with all his household, who gave alms generously to the people, and prayed to God always. ... 31 "...'Cornelius, your prayer has been heard, and your alms are remembered in the sight of God.'" (NKJV)*

See in the next chapter, additional *"Scriptures for Meditation"* under sections: *"For the Good"* and *"What About the Poor."*

Remember, the poor we will always have with us, and...

It's not our money. It's His.

SCRIPTURES FOR MEDITATION

The Corruption of Money

Psalm 52:7 – "Look what happens to mighty warriors who do not trust in God. They trust their wealth instead and grow more and more bold in their wickedness."

Psalm 62:10 – Don't make your living by extortion or put your hope in stealing. And if your wealth increases, don't make it the center of your life.

Proverbs 10:15 – The wealth of the rich is their fortress; the poverty of the poor is their destruction.

Proverbs 11:18 – Evil people get rich for the moment, but the reward of the godly will last.

Proverbs 11:24 – Give freely and become more wealthy; be stingy and lose everything.

Proverbs 15:27 – Greed brings grief to the whole family, but those who hate bribes will live.

Proverbs 20:21 – *An inheritance obtained too early in life is not a blessing in the end.*

Proverbs 28:22 – *Greedy people try to get rich quick but don't realize they're headed for poverty.*

Proverbs 28:25 – *Greed causes fighting; trusting the LORD leads to prosperity.*

In reference to Israel's constant rebellion...
Jeremiah 6:13 – *"From the least to the greatest, their lives are ruled by greed. From prophets to priests, they are all frauds.*

The rebuke of an ungodly king...
Jeremiah 22:17 – *"But you! You have eyes only for greed and dishonesty! You murder the innocent, oppress the poor, and reign ruthlessly."*

Again, speaking of the desolation of Israel...
Ezekiel 7:19 – *"They will throw their money in the streets, tossing it out like worthless trash. Their silver and gold won't save them on that day of the LORD's anger. It will neither satisfy nor feed them, for their greed can only trip them up.*

Habakkuk 2:5 – *Wealth is treacherous, and the arrogant are never at rest. They open their mouths as wide as the grave, and like death, they are never satisfied. In their greed they have gathered up many nations and swallowed many peoples.*

Haggai 1:9-11 *- 9 You hoped for rich harvests, but they were poor. And when you brought your harvest home, I blew it away. Why? Because my house lies in ruins, says the LORD of Heaven's Armies, while all of you are busy building your own fine houses. 10 It's because of you that the heavens withhold the dew and the earth produces no crops. 11 I have called for a drought on your fields and hills--a drought to wither the grain and grapes and olive trees and all your other crops, a drought to starve you and your livestock and to ruin everything you have worked so hard to get."*

Matthew 23:25 *– "What sorrow awaits you teachers of religious law and you Pharisees. Hypocrites! For you are so careful to clean the outside of the cup and the dish, but inside you are filthy--full of greed and self-indulgence!* (also see Luke 11:39)

Mark 7:20-22 *– 20 And then he added, "It is what comes from inside that defiles you. 21 For from within, out of a person's heart,* *come evil thoughts, sexual immorality, theft, murder, 22 adultery, greed, wickedness, deceit, lustful desires, envy, slander, pride, and foolishness.*

Luke 12:15, 20 *– 15 Then he said, "Beware! Guard against every kind of greed. Life is not measured by how much you own..." But God said to him, 'You fool! You will die this very night. Then who will get everything you worked for?'*

In speaking of sinners...

Romans 1:29 *– Their lives became full of every kind of wickedness, sin, greed, hate, envy, murder, quarreling, deception, malicious behavior, and gossip.*

Ephesians 5:3 *– Let there be no sexual immorality, impurity, or greed among you. Such sins have no place among God's people.*

1 Timothy 3:2-4, 8 *– 2 A bishop then must be blameless... 3 not... greedy for money... not covetous; 4 one who rules his own house well... 8 Likewise deacons must be... not greedy for money. (NKJV)*

1 Timothy 6:17 *– Teach those who are rich in this world not to be proud and not to trust in their money, which is so unreliable.*

Their trust should be in God, who richly gives us all we need for our enjoyment.

Titus 1:7 – *For a bishop must be blameless, as a steward of God, not self-willed, not quick-tempered, not given to wine, not violent, not greedy for money. (NKJV)*

James 5:1-5 – *1 Look here, you rich people: Weep and groan with anguish because of all the terrible troubles ahead of you. 2 Your wealth is rotting away, and your fine clothes are moth-eaten rags. 3 Your gold and silver have become worthless. The very wealth you were counting on will eat away your flesh like fire. This treasure you have accumulated will stand as evidence against you on the day of judgment. 4 For listen! Hear the cries of the field workers whom you have cheated of their pay. The wages you held back cry out against you. The cries of those who harvest your fields have reached the ears of the LORD of Heaven's Armies.*

5 You have spent your years on earth in luxury, satisfying your every desire. You have fattened yourselves for the day of slaughter.

Speaking of false teachers...

2 Peter 2:3, 14 – *3 In their greed they will make up clever lies to get hold of your money. But God condemned them long ago, and their destruction will not be delayed. ...*

14 They commit adultery with their eyes, and their desire for sin is never satisfied. They lure unstable people into sin, and they are well trained in greed. They live under God's curse.

For the Good

Psalm 112:9 – *They share freely and give generously to those in need. Their good deeds will be remembered forever. They will have influence and honor.*

Proverbs 22:9 – *Blessed are those who are generous, because they feed the poor.*

Luke 6:30-31 – *30 Give to anyone who asks; and when things are taken away from you, don't try to get them back. 31 Do to others as you would like them to do to you.*

2 Corinthians 9:5-11 – *5 So I thought I should send these brothers ahead of me to make sure the gift you promised is ready. But I want it to be a willing gift, not one given grudgingly.*

6 Remember this--a farmer who plants only a few seeds will get a small crop. But the one who plants generously will get a generous crop. 7 You must each decide in your heart how much to give. And don't give reluctantly or in response to pressure. "For God loves a person who gives cheerfully." 8 And God will generously provide all you need. Then you will always have everything you need and plenty left over to share with others. 9 As the Scriptures say, "They share freely and give generously to the poor. Their good deeds will be remembered forever."

10 For God is the one who provides seed for the farmer and then bread to eat. In the same way, he will provide and increase your resources and then produce a great harvest of generosity in you. 11 Yes, you will be enriched in every way so that you can always be generous. And when we take your gifts to those who need them, they will thank God.

1 Timothy 6:18 *– Tell them to use their money to do good. They should be rich in good works and generous to those in need, always being ready to share with others.*

What About the Poor?

1 Samuel 2:7-8 –7 The LORD makes some poor and others rich; he brings some down and lifts others up. 8 He lifts the poor from the dust and the needy from the garbage dump. He sets them among princes, placing them in seats of honor. For all the earth is the LORD's, and he has set the world in order.

Psalm 113:7-8 – 7 He raises the poor out of the dust, and lifts the needy out of the ash heap, 8 That He may seat him with princes--With the princes of His people. (NKJV)

What About Lending?

Leviticus 25:35-37 –35 "If one of your fellow Israelites falls into poverty and cannot support himself, support him as you would a foreigner or a temporary resident and allow him to live with you. 36 Do not charge interest or make a profit at his expense. Instead, show your fear of God by letting him live with you as your relative. 37 Remember, do not charge interest on money you lend him or make a profit on food you sell him.

Deuteronomy 15:8-10 – *8 Instead, be generous and lend them whatever they need. 9 Do not be mean-spirited and refuse someone a loan because the year for canceling debts is close at hand. If you refuse to make the loan and the needy person cries out to the LORD, you will be considered guilty of sin. 10 Give generously to the poor, not grudgingly, for the LORD your God will bless you in everything you do.*

Psalms 112:5 – *A good man deals graciously and lends; He will guide his affairs with discretion.*

Proverbs 19:17 – *If you help the poor, you are lending to the LORD--and he will repay you!*

Proverbs 28:8 – *Income from charging high interest rates will end up in the pocket of someone who is kind to the poor.*

Matthew 5:42 – *"Give to him who asks you, and from him who wants to borrow from you do not turn away. (NKJV)*

Covenantal Blessings

Deuteronomy 28:1-14 – *1 "If you fully obey the LORD your God and carefully keep* *all his commands that I am giving you today, the LORD your God will set you high above all the nations of the world. 2 You will experience all these blessings if you obey the LORD your God: 3 Your towns and your fields will be blessed. 4 Your children and your crops will be blessed. The offspring of your herds and flocks will be blessed. 5 Your fruit baskets and breadboards will be blessed. 6 Wherever you go and whatever you do, you will be blessed.*

7 "The LORD will conquer your enemies when they attack you. They will attack you from one direction, but they will scatter from you in seven!

8 "The LORD will guarantee a blessing on everything you do and will fill your storehouses with grain. The LORD your God will bless you in the land he is giving you.

9 "If you obey the commands of the LORD your God and walk in his ways, the LORD will establish you as his holy people as he swore he would do. 10 Then all the nations of the world will see that you are a people claimed by the LORD, and they will stand in awe of you.

11 "The LORD will give you prosperity in the land he swore to your ancestors to give you, blessing you with many children, numerous livestock, and abundant crops.

12 The LORD will send rain at the proper time from his rich treasury in the heavens and will bless all the work you do. You will lend to many nations, but you will never need to borrow from them. 13 If you listen to these commands of the LORD your God that I am giving you today, and if you carefully obey them, the LORD will make you the head and not the tail, and you will always be on top and never at the bottom. 14 You must not turn away from any of the commands I am giving you today, nor follow after other gods and worship them.

Psalm 1:1-3 – *1 Blessed is the man Who walks not in the counsel of the ungodly, nor stands in the path of sinners, nor sits in the seat of the scornful; 2 But his delight is in the law of the LORD, and in His law, he meditates day and night. 3 He shall be like a tree planted by the rivers of water, that brings forth its fruit in its season, whose leaf also shall not wither; and whatever he does shall prosper. (NKJV)*

Psalm 37:21-22 – *21 The wicked borrow and never repay, but the godly are generous givers. 22 Those the Lord blesses will possess the land...*

Psalm 37:25-26 – *I have been young, and now am old; Yet I have not seen the righteous forsaken, nor his descendants begging for bread. He is ever merciful, and lends; And his descendants are blessed. (NKJV)*

Psalm 92:12-14 – *12 But the godly will flourish like palm trees and grow strong like the cedars of Lebanon. 13 For they are transplanted to the LORD's own house. They flourish in the courts of our God. 14 Even in old age they will still produce fruit; they will remain vital and green.*

Psalm 107:38 – *How he blesses them! They raise large families there, and their herds of livestock increase.*

Psalm 112:4 – *Light shines in the darkness for the godly. They are generous, compassionate, and righteous.*

Isaiah 32:8 – *But a generous man devises generous things, and by generosity he shall stand. (NKJV)*

Apostolic Grace

Act 4:33 – *And with great power the apostles gave witness to the resurrection of* the Lord Jesus. And great grace was upon them all. *(NKJV)*

Act 11:23 – When he came and had seen the grace of God, he was glad, and encouraged them all that with purpose of heart they should continue with the Lord. *(NKJV)*

Act 13:43 – Now when the congregation had broken up, many of the Jews and devout proselytes followed Paul and Barnabas, who, speaking to them, persuaded them to continue in the grace of God. *(NKJV)*

Act 14:26 – From there they sailed to Antioch, where they had been commended to the grace of God for the work which they had completed. *(NKJV)*

Act 15:40 – but Paul chose Silas and departed, being commended by the brethren to the grace of God. *(NKJV)*

Act 20:24, 32 – 24 "But none of these things move me; nor do I count my life dear to myself, so that I may finish my race with joy, and the ministry which I received from the Lord Jesus, to testify to the gospel of the grace of God. ...

32 "So now, brethren, I commend you to God and to the word of His grace, which is

able to build you up and give you an inheritance among all those who are sanctified. (NKJV)

As stated by the Apostle Paul:

1 Corinthians 15:10 – *But by the grace of God I am what I am, and His grace toward me was not in vain; but I labored more abundantly than they all, yet not I, but the grace of God [which was] with me. (NKJV)*

2 Cor 1:12 – *For our boasting is this: the testimony of our conscience that we conducted ourselves in the world in simplicity and godly sincerity, not with fleshly wisdom but by the grace of God, and more abundantly toward you. (NKJV)*

2 Corinthians 8:9 – *You know the generous grace of our Lord Jesus Christ. Though he was rich, yet for your sakes he became poor, so that by his poverty he could make you rich.*

Ephesians 3:7 – *By God's grace and mighty power, I have been given the privilege of serving him by spreading this Good News.*

Philippians 4:11-13 – *11 Not that I was ever in need, for I have learned how to be content with whatever I have. 12 I know* *how to live on almost nothing or with everything. I have learned the secret of living in every situation, whether it is with a full stomach or empty, with plenty or little. 13 For I can do everything through Christ, who gives me strength.*

Spirit of Elijah

***Malachi 4:5** – Look, I am sending you the prophet Elijah before the great and dreadful day of the LORD arrives.*

***Matthew 11:14** – And if you are willing to accept what I say, he is Elijah, the one the prophets said would come.*

***Matthew 17:10-12** – 10 Then his disciples asked him, "Why do the teachers of religious law insist that Elijah must return before the Messiah comes?" 11 Jesus replied, "Elijah is indeed coming first to get everything ready. 12 But I tell you, Elijah has already come, but he wasn't recognized, and they chose to abuse him. And in the same way they will also make the Son of Man suffer."*

***Mark 9:11-13** – 11 Then they asked him, "Why do the teachers of religious law insist that Elijah must return before the Messiah* *comes?" 12 Jesus responded, "Elijah is indeed coming first to get everything ready. Yet why do the Scriptures say that the Son of Man must suffer greatly and be treated with utter contempt? 13 But I tell you, Elijah has already come, and they chose to abuse him, just as the Scriptures predicted."*

Luke 1:17 *– He will be a man with the spirit and power of Elijah. He will prepare the people for the coming of the Lord. He will turn the hearts of the fathers to their children, and he will cause those who are rebellious to accept the wisdom of the godly."*

KNOW JESUS, KNOW PEACE

The word *peace* is the original Hebrew is *Shalom.* Simply defined *shalom* means *the peace that comes from being whole – whole* meaning *nothing missing, nothing broken.* It is not possible to know true peace without knowing the Prince of Peace, Jesus Christ. When we enter a relationship with the Lord, we find what it truly means to know peace.

Often Christianity is confused with other religions of the world. Yet Christianity is not about *religion* – it is about *relationship.* A relationship with the Lord Jesus Christ brings peace that passes all understanding.

Perhaps you have never known the peace that comes from being whole; the peace that comes from knowing Him. Then this section is designed for you! Perhaps some readers already know Him as Lord but have strayed in their relationship with Him. Let us not drift so far from Him that we cease to intimately experience His wonderful ways.

It is not difficult to enter a relationship with the Savior. Romans 10:9-10 says:

> *... if you confess with your mouth the Lord Jesus and believe in your heart that God has*

121

raised Him from the dead, you will be saved. For with the heart one believes unto righteousness, and with the mouth confession is made unto salvation. It is that simple.

I encourage you to pray this prayer aloud now:

Dear heavenly Father, I come to you in the name of Jesus. I believe He is your Son. He died on the cross for my sins, and You raised Him from the dead. He is now seated at Your right hand. Because I believe, I confess Jesus as my Lord and Savior. I receive Him as my Lord and receive forgiveness for all my sins. According to Your Word, as I believe and confess, I am saved. Thank You, Lord, for saving me and cleansing me with the precious blood of Jesus. Thank You, Lord, for loving me unconditionally. I receive Your love and purpose in my heart to live for You. In Jesus' name, Amen.

If you have prayed this prayer, welcome to the family of God! You are no longer a stranger, but now among the beloved in the Lord.

Please share your good news with us through our publisher: Adoration Press, PO Box 1966, Branson, MO 65615. Let us know what God has done in your life.

ABOUT THE AUTHOR

Deborah B Vogelzang is a penname author who wishes to remain anonymous. She is a humble woman of God who has served the LORD with gladness since her youth. She and her husband have many decades of experience in full-time ministry. In her not-so-anonymous life, she has been mentored by some of the leading ministers of our time. Her insight is trustworthy; her wisdom respected. Jesus is her LORD and Savior and to Him she clings daily.

Author Vogelzang carries a unique ability to bring clarity where there is confusion; to restore order even in chaotic times. As God prepares the church of the LORD Jesus Christ for manifestations of His glory and the great end-time harvest, she has emerged as a clear prophetic voice. In times like these, she can be found with her finger on the pulse of what God is doing in the earth.

To him who has ears to hear, let him hear what the Spirit is saying to the church.

> *Revelation 22:12-13, 17 – 12 "Look, I am coming soon, bringing my reward with me to repay all people according to their deeds.*

13 I am the Alpha and the Omega, the First and the Last, the Beginning and the End."

... 17 The Spirit and the bride say, "Come." Let anyone who hears this say, "Come." Let anyone who is thirsty come. Let anyone who desires drink freely from the water of life.